"Blind Taste Cultural Magazine 8"

Sampling & Savoring

anywhere in the world...

by...

Marco Rixecker

Jean Baptiste Pointe du Sable...

'Summary...'

The following narrative includes excerpts from a collection of testimonies in English entitled "'Wild Onion Soup': 'Sampling & Savoring in Chicago, Illinois, United States'", and from a podcast aired on Radio Aula Mundi entitled "Let's Talk About It Anywhere In The World...", where it is all about people's voices, accents and speech patterns, hand in hand with my own personal anecdotes and observations.

In addition to that, locals and travelers will be allowed to introduce themselves in their respective, often indigenous, languages and dialects, and to speak their minds freely, without any paraphrases or expectations.

So, let the story go on from there ...

'Situations & Snapshots...'

In Etzer Cantave's voice Jean-Baptiste Pointe DuSable's original settlement comes alive and conjures up images of a farmstead with crops, such as corn and potatoes, fruit orchards, the inevitable onions and garlic, and fresh meat. The DuSable Heritage Association in Chicago conducts and promotes research on the pioneer who became the founder of the Windy City.

Everything and everybody from around the world came through the area that would become today's Chicago. And quite a few languages would have been spoken. French was the predominant language of communication at the time. A multitude of indigenous languages could be heard as well, especially Pottowatomie, the language of the tribe by the same name whose homeland DuSable's settlement was located in. Other Native languages would include Ottawa, Ojibwe, and Sauk covering an area between Southern Illinois, Indiana, upstate New York, Ontario, and Quebec. And there would be stimulating talk and cultural exchange as part of which people accepted one another. Cultural diversity was not unique or exceptional, it was the norm and part of daily routine.

Even before we can chat online I can sense sort of a calm about Etzer Cantave. Still, the circumstances of our online interview are somewhat stressful. We start about 25 minutes late just because of his sincere efforts to give me the best sound quality.

I had told him that we might want to use Skype for our interview. But he has issues logging in, insists for a while, and eventually asks me by email if we can switch to Zoom. And, in many respects, we end up being better off that way. Our discussion also benefits from a more convenient and comfortable setting for Etzer whose inherent calmness and intrinsic serenity quickly return.

What helps us through the initial hiccup is that Etzer and I already know each other a little bit and have an idea where this is going in a way. We had already spoken to one another by phone a week earlier, after he had gotten back to me by email asking for an initial phone call.

Etzer Cantave is the president of the Jean-Baptiste Pointe DuSable Heritage Association. Its mission is to inform the general public about the so-called founder of Chicago. In addition to that, the idea is to educate people on the vision of a man who has been ignored for a long time and is still being underestimated as an intellectual.

So, this interview is about setting the record straight and updating information about a pioneer who settled down near the onion fields at the mouth of the Chicago River.

Jean-Baptiste Pointe DuSable was a black man who originally came from Haiti. And he came to the United States as a free man, while slavery was still rampant, and racial stereotypes were common. One can only imagine how difficult it would be for a black man with a foreign accent to get a decent education.

But DuSable was a curious and keen observer.

And he saw that the stinky onion fields that would become today's Chicago were at the crossroads of culture and commerce. So, he settled down and built a farm where nobody wanted to live, not even the local Natives. But Jean-Baptiste Pointe DuSable saw that goods and commodities were shipped through the area from the Caribbean to Canada and back.

Coffee, sugar and rum made their way up north, while animal furs and cod traveled back south. The mouth of the Chicago River at Lake Michigan was a strategic point between the Great Lakes and the Mississippi. So, building a trading post right there was a smart move.

Etzer Cantave calls it 'the triangular commerce between Canada, the Caribbean, and Europe'. And DuSable's homestead and trading post was located at the heart of that international triangle. No wonder Carl Sandburg would end up calling the city built right at that spot the 'crossroads of the nation'.

Everything was shipped through the area. Everybody stopped by. And doesn't that sound like today's Chicago?

Anyway, one thing you could not expect or take for granted, if you ran into Jean-Baptiste Baptiste Pointe DuSable at the mouth of the Chicago River, is to hear English. People spoke several languages, and the predominant European language in the Great Lakes region was actually French. Mix that with DuSable's likely practice of Creole and of several local indigenous languages, and you get a colorful mosaic of wonderful sounds and accents.

Now imagine you sit down at the table in Jean-Baptiste Pointe DuSable's farm, and he invites you to share a meal with him. You'd enjoy some homegrown crops and produce, some fresh meat, and maybe even a bottle of French wine.

I can clearly detect pride and passion in Etzer Cantave's voice when he tells me about DuSable's cultural background and his affinity with the indigenous population of the Lake Michigan, Chicago river area way back when. After all, DuSable ended up marrying a local indigenous woman by the name of Kittahawa, who belonged to the Pottawatomie Nation.

And one of the reasons why Etzer Cantave feels so passionate about that story is that the so-called melting pots of that era were not located in the United States of America, which actually still consisted of 13 British colonies back East.

No, they were located in French-speaking and indigenous language-speaking areas such as Haiti, Quebec, and today's Chicago.

Just the name of the city tells a story about the location of Jean-Baptiste Pointe Du Sable's new home close to the onion and garlic fields at the mouth of the Chicago river. Chicago comes from the Pottawatomie word 'Shikaakwa', which French explorers transcribed as 'Checagou', when they first heard it pronounced by the local Natives.

It means 'stinky onion', or 'smelly onion' referring to the predominant fragrance that turned out to be too prohibitive for any settlement, until Jean-Baptiste Pointe Du Sable came along.

Let's fast-forward now, into today's Chicago, and look at the site where the Chicago River flows into Lake Michigan. A bust of Jean-Baptiste Pointe DuSable commemorates the welcoming pioneer who finally has been recognized as the founder of Chicago. Take a moment and look around, as you stand in Pioneer Court Plaza, a name which also commemorates DuSable. You will see some of the most iconic landmarks of today's Chicago.

So, in Etzer Cantave's voice images of the past are blended with visions of the future.

Jean-Baptiste Pointe DuSable would feel right at home in today's Chicago, especially among all the iconic landmarks near the mouth of the Chicago River; the Tribune Tower, the Wrigley Building, the Magnificent Mile, and the Chicago Riverwalk, where the so-called 'Founder's Trail' allows people to feel like they're following his footsteps in the modern era. And places have been renamed in recognition of the founder of Chicago. There is DuSable Bridge now from which a staircase goes down to the trail along the Chicago River. It offers some outstanding vantage points to admire the city's architecture.

But Etzer Cantave also makes sure that there is no reason to look at things through rose-colored glasses. He points out that Chicago is divided along many different lines, racial lines, economical lines, and even geographical lines between poor suburbs, no-go areas, and fancy neighborhoods with their condos, parks, scenery, and frequently gorgeous views of Lake Michigan.

So, what you can see and experience in today's Chicago is the result of the vision of a man whose cultural heritage Etzer Cantave, the president of the Jean-Baptiste Pointe

DuSable Heritage Association, actually shares. And it reflects cultural diversity and acceptance, as well as different perspectives of history.

No wonder I can detect pride and passion in Etzer's voice. As a matter of fact, I had noticed Etzer's beautiful accent when we spoke on the phone a couple of days before our online encounter. And I knew we were going to discuss the cultural diversity and the linguistic mosaic inherent to a city like Chicago.

Etzer also insists that Chicago has a unique potential and history of acceptance. People from all over the world and of all walks of life do feel welcome in a city that Etzer Cantave wouldn't know so well and love so much if he didn't feel at home as a Haitian-American. It has always encouraged Etzer to express his pride in his home country which has adopted and kept an indigenous name rather than a colonial one, like Saint Domingue.

And its history doesn't start with the abolition of slavery in 1804 either. Etzer makes sure people understand that indigenous cultures and people had lived and thrived on the Caribbean island for ages, long before the arrival of the first Europeans.

It might be one of the reasons why Jean-Baptiste Pointe DuSable was considered almost a chief among the Native People of the area.

But the key reason why Jean-Baptiste Pointe DuSable and the local Natives got along so well is that the pioneer from Haiti was used to cultural diversity and acceptance.

Haitians grow up with the clear notion that the history of their country is not based on the abolition of slavery way ahead of other nations in America, nor does it start with Christopher Columbus. It all began with the first inhabitants on the Caribbean island.

Some Native warriors and leaders are even considered heroes in Haitian textbook history, a refreshing alternative to the Euro-American academic concept of history.

So, Etzer Cantave tries to practice this heritage in today's Chicago with the idea of promoting cultural acceptance and diversity. And it is his cultural background that makes him a true Chicagoan, with its contradictions and conflicts. But the third-largest city in the United States has also stood out as a beacon of potential and possibilities throughout its history.

So, my online conversation with Etzer Cantave conjures up all sorts of images of Chicago in my mind.

They include destinations, attractions, and landmarks like those mentioned earlier. All those iconic places are located on or very close to what used to be Jean-Baptiste Pointe DuSable's settlement at the mouth of the Chicago River.

And the whole narrative comes alive in the voice of a man by the name of Etzer Cantave. He is a great storyteller weaving together the early history of Chicago, the history of Haiti, the general context of North America and Europe in the 18th and 19th centuries, and the biography of a pioneer who became the founder of Chicago. And there is a teaching in that story; cultural acceptance.

That and open-mindedness are fundamental concepts capable of breathing life into any democracy.

As a result, people's perspectives will also change, and they might have, or even work for, a better future, whether it is in Chicago, or anywhere else in the world...

A couple of weeks after my conversation with Etzer Cantave, I do an online interview with a poet, writer and teacher by the name of Shara McCallum. At some point, she and I discuss place names, their origin and meaning. Shara is quite curious about topics like that, because she can associate them with her own cultural roots. Her heritage is Venezuelan and Jamaican, with some other nations from the Caribbean sort of thrown in-between.

So, I mention Jean-Baptiste Pointe DuSable and the meaning of the name 'Chicago' to her, which will cause her to tell me the story about the origin of the name 'Jamaica'.

And the story will go on from there...

'Sites & Sensations...'

...is located at the site where Jean-Baptiste Pointe DuSable's settlement is thought to have been.

Its position near Chicago's Magnificent Mile and the DuSable Bridge and next to the the Tribune Tower and especially the Chicago River make it an ideal starting point for an urban hike along the Pioneer Trail and the Chicago River Walk.

On the plaza itself, the Jean-Baptiste Pointe DuSable Homesite is a designated National Historic Landmark.

Location:

401 Michigan Ave,

Chicago, IL 60611, USA

https://en.wikipedia.org/wiki/Pioneer_Court

"You gotta go to Pioneer Court, and to, see, and, uh, those buildings···

And, to see, uh, the building that I cite, that I cited before···

And, uh, DuSable Bridge···

DuSable Bridge···

And, uh, initially, it was, uh, the Michigan Avenue Bridge, in, to, in 2010, that was renamed, thanks to alderman Riley, I believe, that···

So, it was renamed in honor of DuSable, uh, DuSable Bridge.

And, uh, so, you will cross it. And then, you would go down the stairs, because there is a staircase that takes you from upper, from Michigan Avenue, and then you go down to the, uh, to the Riverwalk.

And that would be what's called the Founder's Trail. The Founder's Trail would be that base, this is where, this···

Basically, the path that he, uh, that, that, uh, where he conducted his business, because, you know···

And so, we call that, uh, it was named after him, uh, in the early 2000's, I believe, uh, Founder's Trail. So, that was to···

And, and further by the lake, and there's the DuSable Harbor. So, these are things that you can really, and, and, and, see. But there's Lakeshore Drive that has been renamed DuSable Drive."

Etzer Cantave,

president of the DuSable Heritage Association

<u>_DuSable Heritage Association..._</u>

...is a non-profit organization whose mission is to

promote the legacy of

Jean-Baptiste Pointe DuSable,

founder of Chicago, through educational

and cultural activities.

"Hello everybody, my name is Etzer Cantave.

I am the president of the DuSable Heritage Association that is dedicated to promoting the legacy of Jean-Baptiste Pointe DuSable, who was the founder of Chicago.

We are located in Chicago, of course."

https://www.dusableheritage.com/

https://www.dusableheritage.com/history

'Sketches & Statistics...'

1780s:

Jean Baptiste Pointe du Sable, a French-speaking settler of African descent supposedly from Quebec, Haiti, or Hispaniola, becomes the first European to settle down near the mouth of the Chicago River and will eventually be recognized as the 'Founder of Chicago' in the mid-20th century.

1795:

On August 3rd, six square miles (16 km^2) of land at the mouth of the Chicago River are reserved for use by the United States in the first Treaty of Greenville, which ends the Northwest Indian War in the so-called 'Ohio Country' and defines the boundary between 'Indian Country and 'Euro-American settlements'. The American delegation headed by General 'Mad Anthony' Wayne includes two members of later fame; Meriwether Lewis and William Clark. The treaty is said to be the reason why Jean Baptiste Pointe du Sable, the 'founder of Chicago', eventually leaves the area.

<u>1796:</u>

Before their departure, Kittahawa, Jean Baptiste Pointe du Sable's Pottawatomie wife, gives birth to Eulalia Pointe du Sable, the first child officially born in what will become Chicago.

<u>'6000':</u>

amount of money in livres for which Jean-Baptiste Pointe Sable sells his property, which includes a farmhouse, 2 barns, a horse-drawn mill, and a baking house, in 1800; the bill of sale will be rediscovered in Detroit in 1913 and will be the official paper that establishes that Pointe du Sable probably is the first non-Native settler in Chicago...

'Sounds & Symbols...'

Jean Baptiste Pointe du Sable

/ʒɑːn bæp'tiːst pɔɪnt du'sɑːbəl/

"(probably born before 1750 died Aug. 28, 1818) is considered the first permanent non-Native American settler of what would later become Chicago, Illinois, which is why he is considered the 'Founder of Chicago'..."

"In the 1780's, he settled near the mouth of the Chicago River at a site that has been designated as a National Historic Landmark, and that is known as Pioneer Court, nowadays located on 401 North Michigan Avenue. Pointe du Sable was of African descent, but little else is known of his life prior to the 1770's, including his birthplace, which several witnesses and historians locate in Quebec, French Louisiana, Haiti, and on the island of Hispaniola. The Chicago area changed hands between France, Britain, Spain, and the United States several times, while he was living there. He married a local Native American woman, Kitiwaha, of the Pottowatomie Nation, and they had two children. In 1800, he sold his land and moved with his family to Saint Charles, Missouri, where he operated a ferry service on the Missouri River."

'Speeches & Specifics...'

"Hello everybody, my name is Etzer Cantave. I am the president of the DuSable Heritage Association that is dedicated to promoting the legacy of Jean-Baptiste Pointe DuSable, who was the founder of Chicago. We are located in Chicago, of course."

Etzer Cantave:

"Please tell us a story about a typical dinner with Jean-Baptiste Pointe DuSable..."

"Okay...

But I'm pretty sure that potatoes would be part of the menu. So, onions for sure...

And I'm pretty sure that, I mean that...

What if DuSable would have invited me over...

I think that, okay...

I would get, I mean, potatoes for sure.

So, he grew crops. So, maybe corn would be part of it, and onions for sure. And he had a smokehouse, you know. His business, his business...

He got a smokehouse; so yeah...

So, I'm pretty sure that we would have a hearty piece of meat there. I mean, I'm pretty sure. And fruits that would be part of it, because he had an orchard too. So, we would have that. Right, so that would be, in my imagination, you know, something typical that I would get. And then, of course, we would have wine, because, in his trading post, he received goods from, from all over, you know. And then, he invited his, uh, he invited some of those traders to stay over, because he built, uh, uh, guesthouses. And I'm pretty sure he had wine there.

So, I would dine to wine as well."

Etzer Cantave:

"What is the last DuSable landmark I should see right before I leave Chicago?"

"Well, Pioneer Court, I mean, you gotta go to Pioneer Court, and to, see, and, uh, those buildings...

And, to see, uh, the building that I cite, that I cited before...

And, uh, DuSable Bridge...

DuSable Bridge...

And, uh, initially, it was, uh, the Michigan Avenue Bridge, in, to, in 2010, that was renamed, thanks to alderman Riley, I believe, that...

So, it was renamed in honor of DuSable, uh, DuSable Bridge. And, uh, so, you will cross it. And then, you would go down the stairs, because there is a staircase that takes you from upper, from Michigan Avenue, and then you go down to the, uh, to the Riverwalk.

And that would be what's called the Founder's Trail. The Founder's Trail would be that base, this is where, this...

Basically, the path that he, uh, that, that, uh, where he conducted his business, because, you know...

And so, we call that, uh, it was named after him, uh, in the early 2000's, I believe, uh, Founder's Trail.

So, that was to...

And, and further by the lake, and there's the DuSable Harbor.

So, these are things that you can really, and, and, and, see.

But there's Lakeshore Drive that has been renamed DuSable Drive."

Etzer Cantave:

**"How would you explain today's Chicago to
Jean-Baptiste Pointe DuSable?"**

"Well, it's a daunting task, because I always picture him coming back, coming back to earth, and see that. And, and then, how he would feel...

Instead of me telling him...

Okay, let's bring him back here...

And see, okay, now, what would he feel?

Well, I think, for one thing, he would be, he would be elated to see the kind of development that, uh, I mean, that Chicago has undergone. He'd be pleased and say, 'That's the vision I had. I see that. I see, okay, these, this vibrant place, you know, you know, this hub for global business, for commerce, commerce, you know, commerce all over.'

That, I would say that, you know.

But, but, how would he feel about anything, I mean, this is when he saw, when he would see the divide in the, in the city, because you have, because, because Chicago is divided along many lines, right?

Among racial lines, right...

Among, I mean, um, uh, economic lines, you know, and the, the haves and the havenots, right...

And geographical lines, and the South Side, the North Side, the West Side, and the East Side, you know...

So, that's the kind of thing that Chicago is as well, you know. It's the city of the majestic Lakefront. It's the city of, a, you know, of those iconic buildings, you know, just splendid, and of these architectural feats, I would say. You can see that. And, on the other hand, you had that.

How do you reconcile that?

How do you reconcile these two?

But I think this is where, uh, DuSable would have agreed with me and said, 'So we need DuSable Park. We need a place like DuSable Park.

We need to go back to our roots, to what I designed in my settlement, because this is, because this is a city that was born of, out of diversity, as I said many times, the city whose destiny is in its diversity.'"

Etzer Cantave:

"Which part of you is Chicago?"

"Which part of me is, is Chicago...

I think I have Chicago in me by the main...

I have DuSable in me. DuSable is in me.

And, uh, okay, DuSable's legacy is Chicago itself. It is Chicago. Whatever happens in Chicago becomes automatically part of that legacy.

Anybody who comes to Chicago, who decided to live in Chicago, you automatically...

It's like, it's like when you came to his settlement, you are embraced. You're that...

So, I'm Chicago. I'm that, you know, I'm part of that...

My history is also the history of the smelling onion place as well. I embrace that, you know.

And then, uh, and, and, uh, and, and there's nothing...

And we feel that when Chicago is in the news, not in unfettering terms, I mean, we feel that in, in, in, uh, in our flesh. We feel that, we feel that, I mean, in our psyche, that, okay, uh...

And, and then, we are rooting for the, uh, for this, for this, this city...

So, we have, we have the city in us.

Okay, so, I have Chicago in myself, in me, because we decided, we decided to live here, regardless of the cold weather. And that's one thing, because we left a warm country. And we decided to come, and that was what DuSable did as well.

He came...

We came to one of the coldest places in the U.S., in the U.S., and decided, and we all decided to stay, that, because we had that connection with that land, we decided, you know, to make it our own as well. So, we, we are Chicago. Yeah, so, we are Haitian-Americans, and we are also Chicagoans."

'Synthesis...'

...

'The act of 'Blind Tasting' can be associated with the practice of 'sampling and savoring' all sorts of meals, drinks, music, attractions and activities, without really knowing too much about them. So, this project is meant to allow a reader or traveler to get a cultural experience just like that. The idea is to help you 'get lost out there'. If something like that happened, you might want to be able to speak with the locals, enjoy their food, listen to their music, and appreciate their arts. And, once you are able to do just that, maybe you're going to raise your arms and exclaim, 'I am happy!'

Such a deep and profound experience of 'cultural immersion' will enrich your journey, no matter what. Eventually, you're even going to 'find your way around'.

'Deliciously Addictive' is a unique guidebook, travel story, and documentary based on the interviews with several 'locals & protagonists' in Peru and anywhere else in the world. Their testimonies will help you discover Peruvian Cuisine. Through their voices, the readers, or audience, are supposed to get a genuine perspective of ancient and diverse culinary secrets. Their experiences will provide you with an intriguing angle to all sorts of dishes and drinks in Peru.

the author...

Marco Rixecker is a freelance writer, reporter, producer, teacher, translator, tour guide, poet, singer and songwriter, and he speaks several languages. He is the author of the 'Blind Taste Cultural Guidebook & Documentary' series, and he is also the creator and founder of Radio Aula Mundi and co-founder of the Aula Mundi International Cultural Center. The name of his company is 'On & Off Road Productions & Travel Services'. In his travels he tends to follow historic roads and itineraries, including the old 'Route 66', the 'Lewis & Clark Trail', and the 'Pan-American Highway'. And he keeps traveling the world...

"And the story

goes on from there..."

Victor Reece, Tsimpsian storyteller,

First Nations, Canada